The Mountaintop

Katori Hall is from Memphis, Tennessee. Her play *The Mountaintop* was first produced to great acclaim at Theatre 503, London, in June 2009, and received a transfer to the Trafalgar Studios, London the following month. It won the Olivier Award for Best New Play in 2010, and opened in Broadway's Bernard B. Jacobs Theatre, New York City, in October 2011.

Her other plays include *Hurt Village* (Classical Theatre of Harlem Future Classics Reading Series, BRIC Studio, 2007), *Hoodoo Love* (Cherry Lane Theatre, New York, 2007), *Remembrance* (Women's Project/World Financial Center site-specific work, 2007), *Saturday Night/Sunday Morning* (Classical Theatre of Harlem Future Classics Reading Series, The Schomburg Center, New York, 2008), *WHADDABLOODCLOT!!!*, *The Hope Well* and *Pussy Valley*.

Her numerous awards include the 2007 Fellowship of Southern Writers Bryan Family Award in Drama, a 2006 New York Foundation of the Arts Fellowship in Playwriting and Screenwriting, a residency at the Royal Court Theatre in 2006, and the 2005 Lorraine Hansberry Playwriting award.

WITHDRAWN

Katori Hall

The Mountaintop

Methuen Drama

Published by Methuen Drama 2011

Methuen Drama, an imprint of Bloomsbury Publishing Plc

1 3 5 7 9 10 8 6 4 2

Methuen Drama
Bloomsbury Publishing Plc
49–51 Bedford Square
London WC1B 2DP
www.methuendrama.com

Copyright © Katori Hall 2011

Foreword copyright © Michael Eric Dyson 2011

Afterword copyright © James Dacre 2010, 2011
Reproduced by permission of the *Independent*

Katori Hall, Michael Eric Dyson and James Dacre have asserted their rights
under the Copyright, Designs and Patents Act, 1988 to be identified
as the authors of this work

ISBN 978 1 408 14703 0

A CIP catalogue record for this book is available from
the British Library

Available in the USA from Bloomsbury Academic & Professional,
175 Fifth Avenue/3rd Floor, New York, NY 10010.
www.BloomsburyAcademicUSA.com

Typeset by Country Setting, Kingsdown, Kent CT14 8ES
Printed and bound in the USA by Edwards Brothers, Inc., Lillington, NC

Caution

Contents

Foreword *by Michael Eric Dyson*

King's Knock at Midnight

It must be stated as clearly and insistently as possible: Katori Hall's *The Mountaintop* is artistic dynamite. It explodes the myths that bury Martin Luther King, Jr.'s humanity and shatters his image as a stoic martyr. *The Mountaintop* invites us to see King as a flesh-and-blood genius with flaws who worked fiendishly to end black oppression while fighting for liberty and justice for all. These pages teem with wisdom about the black, and therefore, the human condition, but it isn't served up in musty language or reverent grammar. The dialogue pops off the pages in vernacular wit and folk philosophy; its lines are laced with humor, irony, paradox, signifying and magic. It's not the sort of magic that rescues us from the grip of grief; rather it's the kind of magic that conquers tragedy by facing it head on. *The Mountaintop* portrays a man who is much more interesting and useful when his blemishes and virtues are shown together.

One might ask why we would turn to the dramatic arts when the best scholarship on King has already warned against smothering him in fable. Sometimes poetry tells more truth about history than either science or religion. Poetry is Hall's greatest weapon in her loving war against the lazy deification of Martin Luther King, Jr. Her words snap and jolt, and at times they even pounce in delicious ridicule of the hollow, deadening worship of King, insisting instead that we take him at his word. Not the immortal words he uttered in public that have won the favor of history, but the words we never got to hear him say, the words that fear pried from his lips, or the words that tumbled from a tongue that depression turned into a staircase of spiraling doubt near the end of his life. That's a side of King that only his closest compatriots glimpsed. And most of them only saw snapshots of King's inner turmoil as the movement for justice lurched in seizures of resistance, sputtering and then taking off again as heroic freedom fighters battled evil in some far-flung corner of the black universe.

Memphis in March and April of 1968 was such a moment. King had been summoned for the umpteenth time to channel – or truth be told, to catch on to – the resurging spirit of a battered movement.

Hall draws a literary circle around the next-to-last day of King's bitterly shortened life, a life, like the movement he led, riddled by chaos and transition. How could it be otherwise? All roads for the Nobel-prize winning evangelist of hope led to death. The government harassed King to death. White supremacists hounded him to death. His followers loved him to death. And King worked himself to death. When the coroner opened his body after a bullet felled the thirty-nine-year-old prodigy of protest, it was his heart that lodged the greatest resistance: it looked to be that of a sixty-year-old man.

This fact makes it way into Hall's drama, as do other telling details which are skillfully woven into the narrative: King's vicious bouts of hiccups, which disappeared when he spoke, and which resumed after his oration was done; King's chain-smoking; his artful and relentless bending of the elbow (and my God why not, given what he was up against?); his vanity about being *the* black leader (so tell all those who compare Jesse Jackson and Al Sharpton unfavorably to King that, at least on this score, they're dead wrong); King sending his wife artificial flowers only once – a few days before his demise, another sign of premonition blooming in his brain; King's fear of flying and, given how much he flew, a fear that underscored his courage; King's haunting anxiety near the end of his life of being in rooms with windows that might present his potential assassin clear opportunity; and King's brutal battle with depression.

Hall may not be a historian, but her art is eerily accurate. She conjures fictional scenes that nourish us with an understanding that dry facts alone starve us of. Hall's dramatic license also opens the door to hotly contested truths that range far beyond King's life and death: the gender of God; how class colors social relations in black life; the belief in an afterlife, and the shape it might take; and the inscrutable ways of God, as Hall's theatrical meditations amount to a grassroots theodicy of sorts.

Hall peers brilliantly into the shadows of King's last night on earth and lights briefly on the monumental speech he pulled from the core of his soul. King's words dripped in death, but Hall convinces us that King wasn't simply addressing his immediate circumstances, but speaking to the specter of imminent death that dogged him most of his life. That's entirely plausible since he was being pursued relentlessly by crackpots, and crack shots, across the land. King is seen here begging off the bravery he displayed in his last speech where he declared he wasn't worried about anything or fearing any man. This doesn't make him a hypocrite, but a man struggling with his mortality. Even Jesus begged God to spare him from drinking the bitter cup of his destiny, a destiny he had previously proclaimed with full readiness to die. But when the moment of death looms near, words of certainty crumble beneath the tangible threat of non-being.

Still, words uttered in higher, clearer moments provide a touchstone of faith to thwart the doubt that inevitably creeps in when the rubber meets the road, when death swagger gives way to death stagger, at least for a while. Besides, only those who know the transcendent heights to which oratory can take you, not only as a hearer but as a giver of the word, can possibly understand how one can literally speak oneself into courage and vision that are less apparent in mundane moments. This is not simply a matter of being whipped into frenzy or driven to flights of fancy by the power of words. Speech gives individuals and societies a sense of who we are, and what we are capable of; words give life, order existence and clarify destiny. 'In the beginning was the Word . . . '

By spotlighting King's last night, Hall illumines our nights too: the time of reckoning, the time of wrestling, like Jacob in the Hebrew Bible, with powerful, wounding forces below, only to discover we were wrestling with a messenger from above. Hall magically sweeps us into King's cramped, pinched, smoky, desolate, and dingy temporary living quarters to show us a picture of a human soul struggling with death – his death, the death of a way of life in the South, the death of personal and vocational hopes and aspirations, and the death of theological certainties and pulpit proclamations. The cussing, smoking and gallows humor are spiritual anesthesia to endure mortal peril – the awareness that one's life is being snuffed out – and from that mixture rises a truth, or perhaps many of them, that costs one's life to learn.

King was profoundly familiar with late night. One of his most famous sermons is 'A Knock at Midnight'. In it, King says, 'You can have some strange experiences at midnight.' Hall proves King right and summons a fateful late-night encounter to imagine her way into his heart and mind as he surrenders his life for a greater purpose. It does no disservice to King, and in fact helps the rest of us, that King's human side gets the long view here. Only a King who has faced his own fears, nursed his own psychic wounds, stirred in private remorse at his own sins, and yes, reveled in defiant mischief, can possibly speak to the masses of folk who will never wear the victor's crown nor taste the sweet adoration of millions. Only a King who has descended to the depths of hell and stared at his own mortality can possibly inspire the rest of us to overcome our flaws and failures and rise to our best futures. The restoration of King to his complicated humanity is way too much to ask of even a work as poignant as *The Mountaintop*. But it is a sign of its dramatic genius that, after reading it and witnessing its performance, it makes us believe that the task is necessary, and that this play is as good a place as any to start the journey.

August 2011

The Mountaintop

For my mother, Camae

The Mountaintop was developed during the Lark Play Development Center Barebones workshop in New York City on April 29, 2009 (John Eisner, artistic director; Michael Roberston, managing director). The cast was as follows:

Dr Martin Luther King, Jr. Jordan Mahome
Camae Dominique Morisseau

Directed by Kamilah Forbes
Stage Manager Stacy Waring

The Mountaintop had its world premiere at Theatre 503, London, on June 9, 2009 (Tim Roseman and Paul Robinson, artistic directors). The cast was as follows:

Dr Martin Luther King, Jr. David Harewood
Camae Lorraine Burroughs

Directed by James Dacre
Set and costume design by Libby Watson
Lighting design by Emma Chapman
Music and sound by Richard Hammarton
Video design by Dick Straker for Mesmer
Deputy stage manager Sarah Jenkins
Assistant director Teunkie van de Slujis
Line producer Davina Shah
Voice and dialect Charmian Hoare
Magic consultant Nick Mohammed
Casting consultants John Manning
　　Annie Rowe
　　Janine Snape
Line producer Davina Shah

This production transferred to Trafalgar Studios, West End, on July 21, 2009 (produced by Sonia Friedman Productions, Jean Doumanian, Tali Pelman for Ambassador Theatre Group, Bob Bartner, Freddy DeMan, Jerry Frankel, Ted Snowdon and Marla Rubin Productions Ltd).

The Mountaintop opened at the Bernard B. Jacobs Theatre on Broadway in New York City on October 13, 2011 (produced by Jean Doumanian, Sonia Friedman, Ambassador Group and Bartner). The cast was as follows:

Dr Martin Luther King, Jr.   Samuel L. Jackson
Camae   Angela Bassett

Directed by Kenny Leon
Set and video design by David Gallo
Costume design by Constanzo Romero
Lighting design by Brian MacDevitt
Sound design by Dan Moses Schreier
Music composition by Branford Marsalis

Characters

Dr. Martin Luther King, Jr.   Thirty-nine, Nobel Peace
Prize-winning civil rights movement leader.

Camae   Twenties, Lorraine Motel maid.

Setting

3 April 1968.
Room 306, Lorraine Motel, Memphis, Tennessee.

Dr. Martin Luther King, Jr retires to room 306 in the Lorraine
Motel after giving a speech to a Memphis church congregation
during the sanitation workers' strike. When a mysterious
young hotel maid comes to visit him during the night, King is
forced to confront his mortality and the future of his people.

Lights up. Night. 3 April 1968. Room 306, the Lorraine Motel, Memphis, Tennessee. The outside street lights project the shadows of rain sliding down the pane on to the walls.

The motel room door creaks open. The rain pours outside. Enter **Dr. Martin Luther King, Jr.** *Tired. Overwrought. Wet. He is ready to take his shoes off and crawl into bed. He coughs. He is hoarse. He stands in the doorway, the red and yellow motel sign casting a glow on to his face. He yells out of the door into the stormy night.*

King Abernathy, get me a pack of Pall Malls, when ya go. Naw. Naw. Naw. I said Pall Malls. I don't like those Winstons you smoke. You can call me siddity all you like, I want me a Pall Mall. Pall Malls, man! Don't be cheap. Be back soon, man. I'm wanting one. Bad. That's right . . . That's right . . .

He closes the door. He locks the deadbolt. Click. He chains the door. Rattle. Then he pulls the curtain tight over the window. He walks around in the darkness, but he knows the lay of the room well. He turns on a lone lamp that instantly illuminates the room. Water stains pockmark the walls. Bright orange and fading brown sixties decor accent the room. The carpet is the color of bile. He loosens his tie. Unbuttons his shirt. Coughs.

An opened briefcase lies on one of the two full beds, covered with rumpled peach sheets. He picks up his sermon papers from the bed.

(Reading.) 'Why America is going to Hell . . . '

He goes into the bathroom.

'Why America is going to Hell . . . '

We hear him urinate. He flushes the toilet. He walks back into the room.

They really gonna burn me on the cross for that one.

'America, you are too ARROGANT!'

He goes to the nightstand and checks the empty coffee cups.

What shall I say . . . what shall I say . . .

He goes to the black rotary phone on the night stand between the beds. He dials.

America . . . Ameri –

He stops. In complete silence: unscrews the receiver. Checks the phone for bugs. None there. Screws the receiver back. Checks the night stand. None there. Sighs. Dials again.

Room service? There's not any more room service, tonight? When did it stop? Last week? We were here last week and y'all were still serving room service till midnight. Been always able to get me a cup of coffee when I wanted it. Needed it. Pardon? I just want a coffee. One cup. (*Pause.*) Thank you! Got to do some work before I go to bed. You can bring it on up. Room 306. (*He smiles a broad smile.*) Yes, we call it the 'King-Abernathy Suite' too. I appreciate that, sir. We thank you for your prayers, sir. We're not gonna stop. These sanitation workers gonna get their due. I'm here to make sure of that. Yes, sir! My autograph, sir? (*Beat.*) Uhhh . . . I don't give those out. I only give thanks. Sorry, sir. Yes. It'll be right up? Five minutes? Thank you kindly. Kindly.

He hangs up. He gives the phone a 'what the fuck was that about' look.

'America, America, my country 'tis of thee . . . '

He begins to take off his shoes.

'My country who doles out constant misery – '

He smells them.

Wooooh! Sweet Jesus. I got marching feet and we ain't even marched yet!

He throws them down. He turns to rifle through his suitcase.

Shit. She forgot to pack my toothbrush again.

He dials on the rotary phone.

(*Singing to himself.*) Corrie, pick up . . . Corrie pick up, Corrie, Corrie, Corrie, pick up . . .

She doesn't. He puts the phone down.

My country who doles out constant misery. War abroad. Then war in your streets. (*Under his breath.*) 'Arrogant America.' What shall I do with bbbbbb –

He throws himself back on the bed. There is a knock at the door. He rushes to go and answer. He undoes the deadbolt, then the chain.

Reverend, about time, man. The store ain't but down the street –

Enter **Camae**, *a beautiful young maid. She stands in the doorway, one hand holding a newspaper over her head to catch the rain, the other balancing a tray with a cup of coffee.*

Camae   Room service, sir.

King   That was fast.

Camae   Well, I been called Quickie Camae befo'.

He is taken aback, stunned by her beauty. She waits and waits and waits. He snaps out of it.

King   Where are my manners? Come on in.

He steps aside. She walks in. Dripping over everything.

Camae   Where would you like me to put this?

King   On the table over there.

She sets the tray on the downstage table, bending slightly at the waist. **King** *appreciates his view. Beat. She looks back; he looks away.*

King   How much is that gonna cost?

Camae   Folk down there say it's on the house. For you. It like this yo' house, they say. So you ain't gotta pay them. But you *can* pay me a tip for gettin' my press 'n curl wet out in this rain.

She holds out her hand. He smiles and pulls money from his billfold.

King   You new?

Camae   First day, sir.

King   That's why. I haven't seen you before. Stayed here plenty a' times, but I've never seen your face.

Camae   I done seen yo's befo' though.

King   Oh, have you?

Camae   Of course. On the TV down at Woolworth's. You like the Beatles.

King   Wish folks would listen to me like they listen to the Beatles.

Camae   Mmhm. 'Specially white folks.

King *laughs, then breaks into a fit of coughs.*

Camae   Sound like you needin' some tea, not no coffee. You got a cold?

King (*straining*)   Just done got to getting hoarse. Shouting.

Camae   And carryin' on.

King   No, not carrying on. Testifying.

Camae   Shame I ain't get a chance to see ya tonight. I heard you carried on a storm up at Mason Temple.

King   How you know?

Camae   Negro talk strike faster than lightnin'. They say folks was all cryin'. Sangin'. Mmph. Mmph. Mmph. I woulda liked to have seen that. Somethin' to tell my chiren. 'When I wun't nothin' but a chick-a-dee, I seen't Dr. Martin Luther Kang, Jr cuttin' up in the pulpit.' Mmmhmm. I bet that was somethin' to see.

King *goes to peek out of the window.*

King   Wish it had been more folks there.

Camae   How many was there?

King   Mmmm. A couple thousand.

Camae   Honey, that a lot.

King   Coulda been more in my humble opinion.

Camae   But it was stormin'. Tornadoes and all get out. You can't get no Negro folks out in no rain like this.

King   And why is that?

Camae   God'll strike you down if you move 'round too much. That what my momma used to say. When it storm like this my momma'd say, 'Be still!' But I thank she just wanted us chiren to sit our tails down somewhere 'cause the lightnin' spooked her nerves so bad. Personally, I just thank God be actin' up.

King   Do He? Is that why *you* didn't come?

Pause. She wants to say something, but changes her mind.

Camae   Naw. It my first day here. At work. Wanted to come in early.

King   Well, I can't blame folks. Shoot, *I* almost didn't go.

Camae   Why that?

King   Ain't been feeling too good.

Camae   Aww, a little sick?

King   You could say that . . . Personally, I don't think God's what kept folks in their houses tonight. Folks just don't care.

Camae   Folks 'fraid of gettin' blown up. Churches ain't even safe for us folks.

Thunder and lightning. Boom. Boom. Crackle! **King** *jumps slightly.*

Camae   You . . . all right?

King (*fidgeting*)   Sure . . . sure.

Beat. She goes stage left, checks the bathroom. Takes some wet towels out and slings them across her shoulder.

Camae   You need anythang else 'fore I go?

King   Actually . . . if you got a cigarette . . .

Camae   Cigarettes *and* coffee? That ain't a diet befittin' of a preacher.

King   'Judge not and ye shall not be judged.'

Camae   Honey, I hears that. I guess if you was at home you'd be eatin' mo' right.

King   I suppose.

Camae   What you miss the most she make?

King   Her egg sandwiches.

Camae   Mmm. I likes them, too. Make one every day for myself.

She pulls out a pack of cigarettes. Offers him one. He takes it gladly. Looks at it closely. Staring her down, he puts it in his mouth. She takes out a lighter. Lights it for him.

King   Not too many women running 'round smoking Pall Malls. Impressive.

Camae   Quite. My daddy smoked Pall Malls. Said Kools'll kill ya.

King   Have yourself one.

Camae   What?

King   Smoke one with me.

Camae (*smiling*)   Nah, nah, Preacher Kang. You 'bout to have my boss up after me. I don't know what the rules is yet. Don't know where the dark corners in this place is to hide and smoke my Pall Malls. Don't even know which rooms to lay my head for a quick nap.

King   What about this one?

Beat. She looks at the bed.

Camae   Last folk up in here was doin' the hoochie coochie for pay. I wouldn't lay down in that bed if somebody paid me.

King   So what kinds of rules does a little lady like you break?

Camae   None that involve no preacher, I tells ya that.

King   Everybody should break a rule every now and then.

Camae   Yessir. I's agrees witcha. But not tonight . . . *Not* tonight.

King   Have one wit' me. They're not gonna come looking for you.

Camae (*laughing nervously*)   You the one gone get caught. Kidnappin' me like this.

King   Just one. Till my friend come back with my pack.

Beat. She sighs. She takes a cigarette out and lights it. Inhales. Lets it all out. They look at each other.

Camae   You sho'll do try hard at it.

King   Well . . . you're pretty.

Camae   I know. Even my uncle couldn't help hisself. You have fun tonight?

King   Fun?

Camae   It gotta be fun. Otherwise you wouldn't do it.

King   Not any fun in this.

Camae   Sound like grand fun to me. Standin' up there in the middle of them great big old churches. People clappin' for you. Fallin' out. (*To herself.*) Must be muthafuckin' grand to mean so much to somebody. Shit, *goddamn* must be grand. (*Beat.*) Where a needle and thread to sew up my mouth? Here I is just a' cussin' all up in front of you, Dr. Kang. I cuss worser than a sailor with the clap. Oooo, God gone get me! I'm goin' to hell just for cussin' in front of you. Fallin' straight to hell.

He laughs.

King   No ma'am, 'cordin' to your face, you done fell straight from heaven.

He sips his coffee.

Camae   You lil' pulpit poet you. I likes you.

King   I likes you, too.

The phone rings.

Excuse me.

Camae   Well, I'll just be on my –

*He motions for her to stay. Then puts on his '**King** voice'.*

King   Dr. King, here. (*Voice shifts.*) Oh, Corrie. Yes. I did call.
You didn't pick up. Oh. You were at a meeting. Oh. It went
fine. Not as many people there, but . . . it was enough. I am
getting hoarse, I know. Yes, I'm drinking my tea. I'm drinking
tea right now.

*He looks at **Camae**, who snickers. He motions for her to be quiet.*

King   You know you forgot to pack my toothbrush? Yeap.

He laughs, checks his breath.

I'll just get another one in the morning. Don't worry, darling.
You can't remember everything. (*Silence.*) Did they call? What
they say this time? Hmm. Hmm. Ugly voices. Mmph. You
worried? I'm not.

He takes a long drag on his cigarette.

The children asleep? Oh. *She* still up. She shouldn't be up so
late past midnight. Oh, she can't sleep. Well, let me talk to her.
(*Pause.*) Hey, it's Paw. Mmmhmm. What Paw say? You have to
listen to your Ma when Paw's not there. Yes. You having
trouble sleeping? Me too, sometime. You know what I do? I
just lay down and pray for a bit and that makes me nod off in
no time. It makes everything real peaceful. You promise you
gonna be good? Okay, let Paw speak to your Ma. Oh. She's in
the bathroom, now? Just tell Yolanda and the boys Paw'll see
'em when I get back. Tell Maw I love her. Goodnight, Bernice.

He hangs up the phone.

Camae   You shouldn't lie like that.

King   Like what?

Camae   About drankin' tea. Lyin' tail.

King   Coffee can't cure a cold, can it?

Camae   Coffee wit' some whiskey in it can.

She pulls out a flask and casts a dollop into his cup.

This what the Irish call 'cough syrup'.

King *laughs heartily.*

Camae   She's beautiful. Yo' wife. I seen't her on the TV down at Woolworth's, too. Corretta Scott K –

King *(correcting)*   *Mrs.* King.

Camae   Oh. Yes. *Mrs.* King.

He drinks his coffee.

King   The color of coffee with a lot of milk and a lot of sugar. Just how I like it.

Camae   Well, I likes my coffee black and bitter.

He looks at the name tag on her chest.

King   'Carrie Mae'. That's not what you said earlier.

Camae   Folk shorten it. Call me Camae.

King   Carriemae?

Camae   Naw, naw, na! CA–MAE. Camae.

King   Doesn't make any sense.

Camae   It do too. Say it wit' me. *(Slowly.)* Camae.

King   Cammmae.

Camae   Camae!

King *(teasing)*   CAR–mae?

Camae   CAMAE!

King (*laughing*)   Camae!

Camae (*laughing too*)   Right! Right! There ya go. Sound good comin' outcho mouth.

King   A lot of things do.

Camae   Sho'll do.

King   Sho'll do.

Beat.

Camae   Well, you axe for me if you need anythang else. Just pick up the phone and give me a hollah. The switchboard man'll get me.

King   I can ask for you especially?

Camae   If me is what you want.

Beat.

King   Alrighty then.

Camae   Alrighty then.

She slowly makes her way to the door. She looks back to him. Smiles. She opens the door. The storm has gathered more fury outside. BOOM, BOOM. BOOM!!

King (*stuttering*)   C-c-can I ask you a question before you go? And you promise to answer me open and honest?

Camae   Depend on what the question is.

King   You won't think me less of a man, if I ask?

Camae   I might.

King   I've been needing a woman's perspective on this.

Camae   Like I say, it depend on the question. Shoot.

She closes the door. Beat.

King   Do you think I should shave my mustache?

Beat.

Camae   Yes. I was just sayin' that to myself just then, 'He look so damn ugly with that mustache.'

King   Really?

Camae   Naw! I thought you was gone ask me about somethin' mo' important than that.

King   That is important! My physical appearance is important. To the people.

Camae   Gone on somewhere wit' that!

King   I'm serious! Tell me the truth. Moustache or no mustache?

He covers his mustache with his hand, then uncovers and covers again.

Mustache or no mustache? Mustache or no mustache?

Camae (*laughing*)   Where is that man witcho Pall Malls so you can stop axin' me crazy questions?

King   I don't know where Ralph is. I just thought I'd get a woman's opinion.

Camae   Well, have you axed yo' wife?

Beat.

King   No.

Camae   Well, axe her then. She the one supposed to make them kinds of decisions anyway.

King *goes to the mirror downstage and peers at his face.*

King   Just tryin' to shave some years off. I done got to looking old.

Camae   You have. You look older. In person. When women get older, they get ugly. When men get older they get . . . handsome. Wrinkles look good on a man. Especially when they got some money to go wit' they wrinkles.

King   Women do like men with wrinkles, don't they?

Camae   I don't. I likes 'em young and wild. Like me.

King   Like you?

Camae   Yes, Preacher Kang.

King (*smiling at the memory*)   I used to be young and wild myself.

Camae   You a preacher. That's part a' y'all job requirement. How you know what you ain't supposed to do if you ain't done it, yaself? Folk won't listen to you otherwise. That what I call 'work experience'. More than qualify ya for the position.

King   And what qualify you to be a maid?

Camae   I'm betta at cleanin' up other folks' messes than my own. I was called to do this.

King   Well. I think I was, too.

He sees that his cigarette is finished.

Can I have another one?

Camae   You ain't gone leave me here to work through the night wit nothin' to smoke on. Shhhh-iiii – oooot! All I got is one square left.

King   Perhaps we can share?

He moves closer to her. Beat.

Camae   Like, I say, you *sho'll* try hard at it.

He holds his hand out.

King   Well, the spirit is willing, but the flesh is weak.

As she speaks the following, she hands him her last cigarette. Lights it for him. Then throws her empty pack into the trash can.

Camae   Mmph, mmph, *mmph*! These goddamn folk got you chain smokin' harder than a muthafucka.

Beat.

There I go! Got to cussin' again. I am so sorry, Preacher Kang.
I am *so sorry*. I should be shamed of myself. God gone get me
for that one, too.

King   Don't worry. I forgive you.

Camae   I'm glad somebody do.

They look at each other softly.

King   Well, I guess you got other folks' messes to clean up . . .
I don't mean to keep ya. Don't forget your umbrella.

He hands her the wet newspaper she had brought in.

Camae   Unh, unh. That ain't mine. Thass yours. Boss told
me to bring that up for you. Sorry, I got it wet.

King   Well, I thank ya. Thank ya kindly.

He looks at the newspaper.

April 4th? How'd y'all get tomorrow's paper?

Camae (*shrugs*)   Tomorrow already here.

King (*reads*)   'King Challenges Court Restraint. Vows to
March' – they got that right! This Mayor Loeb calls himself
not allowing these sanitation workers to march. (*To himself.*)
Over my dead body. 'Yesterday two US marshalls sped across
town to serve the Negro leaders with copies of the order. They
found Dr. King and four other defendants at the Lorraine
Motel . . . ' (*He reads further and further.*)

Camae   Folks can send you flowers. Since they know where
you stayin'.

King   That ain't the only thing they can send me. (*Reads.*)
'The city said it was seeking the injunction as a means of
protecting Dr. King . . . We are fearful that in the turmoil
of the moment, someone may even harm Dr. King's life . . .
and with all the force of language we can use, we want to
emphasize that we don't want that to happen . . . ' (*Chuckles to
himself.*) Wish the mayor had jurisdiction over airplanes, too.

You know, Camae, somebody called in a bomb threat on my plane from Atlanta to Memphis today? Thank God they didn't find one.

Camae   Just another day on the job.

King   Mmmhmm.

Camae   Civil rights'll kill ya fo' them Pall Malls will.

Beat. They look at each other. Then laugh really, really *hard.*

King   I like your sense of humor. Like mine . . . morbid.

They laugh harder and harder . . . BOOM! Crickle, CRACK. The thunder rolls. **King** *jumps, terribly frightened.*

(*Slightly embarrassed, laughing it off.*) Wheew! Thought they got me!

He puts his hand over his chest. He begins to breathe hard.

Camae   You all right! You all right!

King   Yes. Yes. I am.

He tries to collect himself.

Camae   Don't tell me a grown man like you 'fraid of lil' lightnin'?

King   No. (*Beat.*) No, that's not what I'm afraid of.

Camae   Oh. The thunder?

King   Yes, the sound. It sounds like –

Camae   Fireworks.

He contemplates this for a spell.

King   Yes. Indeed it does.

Camae   Don't be scurred of a lil' fireworks. I loves me some fireworks. Mama used to take us on down to Tom Lee Park to see the fireworks every Fourth of July.

King   Independence Day.

Camae   That right, y'all bougie black folk call it Independence Day. I can't seem to quite call it that yet.

King   You sho'll is pretty, Camae.

Camae   That 'bout the third time you done tole me that.

King   Second.

Camae   The first time you told me witcho eyes.

King   You saw me?

Camae   Hell, a blind man coulda seen't the way you was borin' holes through my clothes. Awww, you blushin'?

King (*nods his head*)   Which is really hard for a black man to do. I'm embarrassed.

Camae   Shuga, shush. You just a man. If I was you, I'd be starin' at me, too.

King   Well, I guess it's your turn to forgive me.

Camae   Forgiven and forgotten.

King   Thank you, Camae. For the . . . *square*?

Camae   I got some family from Detroit. That what they call 'em up there.

King   So you've been to Detroit? How'd you like it?

Camae   I said I got family from up there. I ain't never been.

King   Don't.

Camae   Why?

King   Negro folks done seemed to have lost their manners up there. Like to riot and carry on.

Camae   Honey, I need to move up there then. 'Cause these white folks down here 'bout to be catchin' flies now the way they be actin wit' Negroes these days. I need to catch the first Greyhound up there. Detroit nigger heaven, you axe me.

King   So are you an honorary Panther?

She growls like a panther, she's pretty good.

Camae   Walkin' will only get you so far, Preacher Kang.

King   We're not just walking; we're marching.

Camae   Whatever it is, it ain't workin'.

King   It doesn't work when you have trifling Negroes who call themselves using a peaceful protest to get a free color television.

Camae   Who done did that?

King   Just last week me and my men organized a march for –

Camae   Them garbage men?

King (*correcting*)   Yes, the *sanitation workers*. Must have been thousands upon thousands of people there. Thousands! Everybody from old men to teenage girls to little boys holding up signs that read, 'I AM A MAN'. Somehow they squeezed me to the front, we linked arms and the march began. 'I AM A MAN! I AM A MAN!' we shouted. Well, we hadn't walked but one block before we heard the sound of glass breaking. I was swept up in a tornado of arms, legs, coughing, mace. I didn't wanna leave those people, Camae. I did not wanna leave them, but . . . my men pushed me into a passing car, and . . . I looked through that back window and saw such blessed peace descend into chaos. (*Beat.*) Don't they know, you can't be marchin' down the street, bust into store windows, and then go get you a free color television. We're marching for a living wage . . . not a damn color TV! It just gives these police an excuse to shoot innocent folks. Like that boy . . . that *sixteen-year-old* boy they shot. Last week? (*Quietly to himself.*) Larry Payne. Larry Payne. Larry Payne. I'll never forget his name . . . Well, we back and we gonna do it right this time. So Larry Payne won't have to have died in vain.

He peeks out of the window, talking as if **Camae** *is not there.*

King   Where is that niggah wit' my pack?

Camae   Maybe he got stuck talkin' wit' some crazy lady in a motel room, too.

King *does not laugh.*

Camae   I'm funny. Laugh.

King   I'm worried. I don't want anything to happen to him. He happen upon something in the night don't know what I'd do without him.

Camae   That your best friend?

King   More loyal than a dog. He the one called me down to the church tonight. Got me out of bed. Just ain't been feelin' right.

Camae *gazes at him softly.* **King** *shakes himself out of it.*

King   He probably downstairs wit' my brother 'nem. Don't like to hang around me too much. I done got to bein' so moody nowadays. 'Forget about last week, Martin,' he says. Forget about it . . . (*He smiles painfully.*) After the march, the papers called me 'Chicken à la King'. Said I was a Commie coward that leaves other people to clean up my mess. 'Martin *Loser* King . . .'

Camae   Seem like times been a little rough on you.

King   Who you telling? Who are you telling . . . (*He peeks out of the window.*) This rain's just relentless. Looking like a monsoon in Memphis.

Camae (*looks at him somberly*)   Well, God ain't gone stop cryin' no time soon.

He hands her his half-smoked cigarette. Beat. She takes it. She takes a long drag between her forefinger and her thumb.

King   You smoke like a man.

Camae   *You* smoke like a fruit.

King   Aww, Camae, don't use those kinda words . . .

Camae   What, you root for the fruits?

King   Indeed I do. Alla God's children got wings.

Camae   Well . . . I agrees witcha on that one. But . . . you just ain't smokin' it right.

King   Well, how am I *supposed* to smoke it?

Camae   Like it's going out of style. Like you need it. Like you want it. That's how I smoke. Make a woman feel sexy. I bet I know why you smoke.

King   Why?

Camae   To feel sexy. 'Cause you look it.

Beat.

King   Aw, Camae. Now, you really makin' me blush. (*Pause.*) I do though, don't I?

Camae   Dr. Martin Luther Kang, Jr. Smoking. Ain't that somethin'? Wish I could take a picture of it.

King   What, you with the FBI?

Camae   Naw. Something bigger.

She hands him back the cigarette. He smokes it like a 'man'. He strikes a sexy pose and blows out a circle ring. **Camae** *pretends to snap pictures.*

There ya go. Just like that. Just like that! Pull harder. Harder. If you want to lead the people you got to smoke like the people. That way the people'll listen to ya.

Beat.

King   You don't think they listen?

Camae   Oh, they listen. They go out and march. Then they get they press 'n curls ruined by fire hoses. Folk done got tired though, Preacher Kang. (*Sighs.*) Like I say, walkin' will only get us so far –

King (*annoyed*)   Well, killin' will get you hung.

Camae   Ain't nobody said nothin' 'bout no killin'. Camae all about ass-whippin's. How about a march for ass-whippin's?

King   That's not gonna do.

Camae   Well, we need to be doin' somethin' else.

King   So what are we supposed to do?

Camae   Somethin'. Somethin' else. Hell, I got bunions and corns for days.

She takes off her shoes and sits down on the bed to rub her feet.

King   Y'all Negroes always want to complain but never have another plan of action. You sound worse than Andy or, better yet, Jesse. Everybody can shoot holes in your ideas, but they can only come up with 'somethin' else'.

Camae   *I* got a plan. But . . . *I'm* just a woman. Folk'll never listen to me.

King   So if you were me, what would you do?

Camae   Really? You wanna know what lil' old me would do?

King   Yes.

Camae   You really wanna know what I'd do?

King   Yes. I. Do.

Beat.

Camae   Can I borrow your jacket?

King   Sure.

Camae   And yo' shoes?

He hands them to her. She puts them on. She stands on top of one of the beds. **King** *looks on in awe. She steadies herself. Throughout her speech* **King** *is her congregation, egging her on with well-timed sayings like, 'Well!' 'Preach!' Or 'Make it plain!'*

Camae (*with a 'King' voice*)   Chuuch! We have gathered here today to deal with a serious issue. It is an issue of great paponderance – you like that? – paponderance! It is a matter of importance more serious than my overgrown mustache: *how do we deal with the white man?* I have told you that the white man is our brother. And he should be treated as such. We touch our brother with the softest of hands. We greet our brothers with the widest of smiles. We give our brother food when he is hungry. But it is hard to do this when our brother beats his fist upon our flesh. When he greets us with 'Nigger' and 'Go back to Africa', when he punches us in our bellies swelling with hunger. Abel was slain by his brother Cain and, just like the Biblical times, today the white man is killing his Negro brethren, shackling his hands, keeping us from rising to the stars we are booooouuuuund to occupy. We have walked. Our feet swelling with each step. We have been drowned by hoses. Our dreams being washed away. We have been bitten by dogs. Our skin forever scarred by hatred at its height. Our godly crowns have been turned into ashtrays for white men at lunch counters all across the South. To this I say, my brethren, a new day is coming. I'm sick and tired of being sick and tired, and today is the day that I tell you to KILL the white man! (*Sotto voce.*) But not with your hands. Not with your guns. But with your miiiind! (*Back to regular voice.*) We are fighting to sit at the same counter, but *why*, my brothers and sisters? We should build our own counters. Our own restaurants. Our own neighborhoods. Our own schools. The white man ain't got nothin' I want. Fuck the white man! *Fuck* the white man! I say, FUCK 'em!

Camae *looks to* **King** *sooooo embarrassed.*

Camae   I AM SO SORRY! Preacher, Kang. Ooooooo. I just can't control my mouth.

King   Obviously, neither can I.

She steps down off the bed. And begins to pull off his jacket.

Camae   Well, you axed. That's what I would say . . . *if* . . .
I was you.

King   That's what you would have me say?

Camae   Why not?

King   'Fuck the white man'? (*Long heavy beat.*) I likes that.
I think that'll be the title of my next sermon.

Camae   Oooooo! Folks ain't gone know what to do with
that.

King   Amen! Fuck 'em!

Camae   I never thought I'd hear you say that!

King   Ooooo! They got me so tired, Camae. All this rippin'
and runnin', rippin' and runnin' around this entire world, and
for what? FOR WHAT? White folks don't seem to want to
listen. Maybe you're right. Maybe the voice of violence is the
only voice white folks'll listen to. (*He coughs.*) I'm tired of
shoutin' and carryin' on, like you say. I'm hoarse.

He grabs **Camae**'s *flask and drinks.*

King   Sometimes I wonder where they get it from. This
hatred of us. I have seen so many white people hate us,
Camae. Bombin' folks' homes. Shootin' folks . . . blowin' up
children.

Camae   Make you scared to bring a Negro child into this
world the way they be blowin' 'em up.

King   Yes, Camae! They hate so easily, and we love too
much.

Camae   Last time I heard you was preachin' 'everybody the
same'. Negro folk. White folk. We all alike.

King   Well, at the most human level we *are* all the same.

Camae   What one thing we all got in common?

Beat. He searches hard to come up with an answer.

King   We scared, Camae. We all scared. Scared of each other. Scared of ourselves. They just scared. Scared of losin' somethin' that they've known their whole lives. Fear makes us human. We all need the same basic things. A hug. A smile. A –

Camae   Smoke?

King (*frustrated*)   Which I could use one more of. Where is that niggah wit' my pack?

Camae *goes to the window, but can't see past the rain.*

King   He always out there runnin' his mouth. Worse than me sometimes. You see him?

Camae   Naw.

King   He'll be back. He know I don't like to be alone too long . . .

Beat. He looks back towards **Camae**.

King   I just wish you had another one. To share, of course.

Camae *pulls another pack of Pall Malls from her maid's uniform.* **King** *stands confused.*

King   I thought you gave me your last one?

Camae   I did. But I'm a magician. I got more where that came from.

King   More tricks up your sleeve?

Camae   Well, as you can tell . . . I ain't yo' ordinary ole maid.

He looks her up and down.

King   Certainly. Certainly! Not too many maids spouting off well-formed diatribes like that.

Camae   What, you thank us po' folk can't talk? You thank we dumb?

King   Naw, naw, that's not what I said, now –

Camae   You thank you always gotta talk for us?

King   No, that's not what I said –

Camae   Then what you sayin'?

King   I'm sayin' . . . that most maids don't sound like professors.

Camae   Well, let me school you, you bougie Negro. I don't need no PhD to give you some knowledge, understand. Divinity school? *Huh!* You don't know who you *messin' wit'*!

King   Well, Camae, I just . . . I just like ya style. Didn't mean to offend ya. Just wanted to compliment ya. You sang it real pretty.

She calms down.

Camae   Well . . . tell me . . . how are my 'oratorical skills' – see ye'en thank I knew them words – How are my *oratorical skills* compared to –

King   Mine?

Camae   Sho.

Beat.

King   I'm better.

Camae   Awww, really, now?

King   You made it sound real pretty, now, but really . . . *I'm* better. Nobody can make it pretty like me. I've been doing this for years, darlin'. Gonna be doin' it till the day I die.

Camae   But was it good?

King   For a woman, yes.

Camae   And if I was a man?

King   Then you'd be Malcolm X.

Camae   So, you callin' Malcolm X a sissy?

King   No, that's not what I said, Miss Camae.

Camae   You callin' Malcolm X a sissy!

King   No, I'm not, Camae.

Camae   I'ma tell it on you!

She runs and opens up the door and screams at the top of her lungs into the pouring night sky.

MALCOLM, MARTIN THANK YOU A SISSY!!!

King   CAMAE! Come from out that door! / You gone get STRUCK!

Camae   You hear that, Malcolm! He callin' you A SISSY!!

The thunder rolls and **Camae** *laughs at the sky threatening to crackle again.*

(*To Malcolm in the sky.*) I'd strike him down for that, too, if I was you.

King *grabs her by the waist and slams the door.*

King   Didn't your mama teach you how to be still when it's thundering and lightning?

Camae   Didn't I tell you I was hard-headed and ain't mind her one bit?

King   Well, God don't like to be laughed at.

Camae   Why? I laugh at God all the time. God funny as Hell. God a fuuuunnny-ass muthafucka.

Beat.

King   I don't like the way you talk about God. You might need to leave you blasphemin' God like that.

Beat.

Camae   I was just tryin' to make you laugh. Bring a little laughter to your life. I like makin' folks laugh, Preacher Kang. God knows you need it –

King   I don't mind laughin'. I like a good joke. Got to. Nowadays. I just don't like how you talk about God.

Camae   I'm sorry. God don't mind it. God ain't like siddity folk. God even like dirty jokes.

King   How you know what God like?

Camae   'Cause I do. I know God liked Malcolm X. And you woulda liked him, too. He didn't drank. Smoke. Cuss. Or . . . Cheat. On. His Wife.

Beat.

King (*wryly*)   And how are you privy to this information?

She stares him down.

Camae   Like, I said befo', Negro talk strike faster than lightnin'. (*Pause.*) Did you ever meet him?

King   Once. But we never got a chance to really –

Camae   Talk?

King   Before he got –

Camae   Killed? (*Pause.*) That's a shame.

King   He was only thirty-nine. (*To himself.*) I'm thirty-nine . . .

Pause.

Camae   He in heaven.

King   Is that right?

Camae   You'll see him there . . . One day.

King   Camae, you talk a lot of nonsense sometimes.

Camae   Nonsense comin' out of a pretty woman's mouth ain't nonsense at all. It's poetry.

King   No, I think that's – what would yo' kinda folk say – *bullshit*?

Camae   Oooooo, I likes it when ya feathers get ruffled. You get all blunt. It look cute on you. But you will. In heaven.

King   So you think he in heaven right now?

Camae   Why wouldn't he be?

King   I don't know, now. He talked a lot of –

Camae   Truth?

King   A lot of violence. He had a weakness for violent words. Speak by the sword, die by the sword –

Camae   Speak by love, die by hate. (*Pause.*) We all have weaknesses, Preacher Kang. I'm sho' you got yo' own. Just ain't never let nobody . . . know. (*Beat.*) For what it worth, I know God like *you*. The real *you*.

King   Do He really?

Camae   *She* likes you.

King   *She?*

Camae   She told me She like you. That if you was in heaven, you'd be her husband.

King (*smiles a big toothy grin*)   Oh, Camae! Is that what God said?

Camae   Yeap.

King   So God in love with me?

Camae   She ain't 'in love', She 'in like'! In like with her some Dr. Kang.

King   I think God ain't told you nothin'. I think it's you who want me for yo' husband.

Camae   Mmmm. Me and God ain't got the same taste. I don't like no man wit' no smelly feet.

King   They do stink, don't they? Don't tell nobody.

Camae   Honey, yo' shoes off. I thank the whole world know by now. Who woulda thunk Dr. Kang got stanky feet. Oooo! And you got holes in yo' socks, too?

King *laughs at her. At himself.*

King   You make it easy.

Camae   Make what easy?

King   To make a man forget about it all. About . . . all . . . this . . .

Camae   That what I'm here for.

King   What else you here for?

He has begun to take off his tie. He struggles a bit. He's gotten stuck.

Camae   What, you tryin' to lynch yoself? Here let me help ya.

They stand face to face. Close. **Camae** *slowly untangles him from it. He stares into her face. Transfixed. He reaches up to touch her face. She smiles.*

King   Thank you.

Camae   You welcome.

BOOM! BOOM! Crickle! CRACK! **King** *stumbles back in a daze. Faint. He begins to hold his chest.*

Camae   You awright?

King   I can't breathe.

Camae   Well, I've been known to have that effect on mens.

King   No, I mean. I can't. I can't / can't, can't can't breathe.

Camae   Oh, my God. Oh, God! / Did I do something wrong?

King   I can't can't can't / breathe. I can't breathe.

Camae   Oh, my God! I did / something wrong! I did something!

King   Can't can't / can't can't can't can't breathe . . .

Camae   Just look into my eyes./ Just look right there.

King   I can't. I can't. I can't.

Camae   Michael?

King   Can't can't / can't −

Camae   Michael! Michael! MICHAEL!! Michael, just breathe!

King (*sotto voce*)   − can't can't / can't can't . . .

Camae   I'ma get you through this. I'ma get you through this night.

Just as soon as it starts, the thunder in **King**'s *heart stops, and he sits stunned, staring at* **Camae***. Silence. They breathe together . . . in . . . out . . . in . . . out . . . in . . . out . . . in . . .*

King   You called me Michael.

Camae (*knowing she did*)   I did?

King   Yes. You. Did. You called me Michael.

Camae   You − you − scared me −

King   How would you know that?

Camae   Know what?

King   To call me that?

Camae   Call you what?

King   YOU KNOW WHAT THE HELL I'M TALKING ABOUT.

Camae   Calm, down Mich − I mean, Preacher Kang. I didn't mean to call you out yo name −

King   But that *is* my name. My childhood name. How do you know my real name? My Christian name?

He slowly backs away from her.

(*Softly.*) Oh. So, you one of them, huh?

Camae   I'm so sorry. I never wanted to do this. This is so hard for me to do −

King (*shaking his head*)   An *incognegro*. A spy.

Camae   I was sent to −

King   WHAT? Tempt me?

Camae   Hell, you was the one tempting me, getting me all off my job!

King   I don't wanna hear it. Get out.

Camae   No.

King   I said get out. You spook.

Camae   I was only doing my job −

King   I said GET OUT! Coming in here tempting me!

Enraged, **King** *overturns the furniture, searching for bugs he may have glossed over.*

Camae   Preacher Kang!

King (*yelling to no one in particular*)   What, y'all think you can trap me again! Record me with a woman, again! Well, you're not going to catch me again!

Camae   Preacher Kang, stop / acting so paranoid!

King   Sending tapes to my wife. Tryin' to break up my family. Tryin' to break my spirit!

Camae   Preacher Kang, calm down!

King   You think you can break me! (*Screaming to no one in particular.*) Well, *you* can't break me! You WILL NEVER BREAK ME AGAIN!

King *grabs* **Camae** *by her arm and aggressively pulls her towards the door.*

Camae   You're hurting me! Preacher / Kang, you're hurting me!!

King   How much they pay you, you *spook*? How much?

Camae   Let go, you're hurting me!!!

King   Where the hell is Ralph? Ralph! I got a spook!

Camae   You wrong! You wrong!

King   Where in the *hell* is Ralph?

HEY!

He opens the door. A wall of snow covers the doorway.

HEEEeeeey . . .

A huge gust of wind blows in snow that piles at his feet. He lets go of **Camae***'s arm. He stands in awe. Looking at the snow.*

King   It's snowing . . . in April.

Camae   It snow sometimes in spring. Here. In Memphis.

He looks back at her. He looks back at the snow at his feet. He looks back at her again. Beat. He closes the door. Then opens it again. He blinks.

King   It's still there. The snow. It's still there.

Camae   As it should be.

He closes the door again.

King   No, no, no, I'm just tired. I'm tired. I'm seeing things that ain't there.

Camae   Oh, it's there.

King   No, it's not. Tell me it's not.

He pulls the curtains back from the windows. They, too, are filled to the brim with snow.

Camae   See, it's there.

King   No. No. No. You've drugged me. Slipped something in my coffee. Some hippie pills in my coffee! Got me seeing things that ain't there.

Camae   I just put some whiskey up in there to relax you –

King   You put some hippie pills in my coffee! Made me see. Snow. Snow? Snow . . .

He opens the door again and sees the snow is still there. His heart threatens to jump out of his chest.

I can't can't can't go anywhere. I can't get out. I can't get *out*!

Camae   Relax! *Calm down!*

He rushes to the phone. Picks it up.

King   Help! HELP! No dial tone.

Camae   Michael!

King   Quit calling me that! QUIT CALLING ME THAT!!

Camae *lunges toward him. He jumps over the bed.*

Camae   We need to calm you down! You gone give yoself a heart attack. You might be thirty-nine but you got the heart of a sixty-year-old man.

King   I can't can't can't go. I can't can't.

He backs himself against the wall.

Camae   Michael! / Shhhhh!!

King   How do you know so much about me! Who in the Hell are you? WHO IN THE HELL ARE YOU?

Camae *blows on the end of a cigarette. It lights up.* **King** *stands stunned. Looong aaaass beat.*

King   Wow.

Camae   I know. Angel breath is some hot breath.

King   You're. An. Angel?

Camae   In the flesh.

King   So, where are your wings?

She points to her breasts.

Camae   These'll get me anywhere I need to go.

King   Wow. An angel?

Camae   Yes. I'm here to take you to the other side.

King   The other side. So I'm not dead?

Camae   No. Not yet.

Beat.

King   Wheew! 'Cause I was about to get mad if heaven looked like this.

They look around the room that's been torn apart in their tussle.

(*Suddenly very serious.*) I'm not going to hell, am I?

Camae   Naw. Naw. Naw! Heaven is where we headed.

King (*with wide eyes*)   Good. Good. Good. Do all angels look as good as you?

Camae   Yes.

King   Heaven must be mighty nice then. I wonder what the women in hell look like?

Camae   Honey, they finer. Why you thank they in hell?

King   Camae, you're really an angel?

He looks at her incredulous. She nods her head.

Camae   Sorry, I called you Michael. Not too many folk prolly know that 'bout you. God said that yo Christian name kinda calms you. Ralph call you that, too. Calms you down quick fast. It a nice name. It ain't better than Camae, though.

King   I changed it / when my daddy did.

Camae   When yo daddy did. When you was just five. I done read yo file. But I don't know why y'all wanna be named after some Martin Luther though. I met him in the cafeteria today and he was kinda weird. Very.

He slowly circles **Camae**.

King   You're really an angel?

Camae   What else I got to do for you to believe me? Cry flowers?

King   But but – but why God send *you*?

Pause.

Camae   What you mean by that?

King   Why He –

Camae   *She!*

King   *She* send you? You're not what I was expecting.

Camae   Shiiiit, you wun't what *I* was expecting, *Preacher* Kang!

King   Well, I'm not perfect.

Camae   That you ain't!

King   Hey, hey, don't judge me, you cussin', fussin' drankin' angel!

Camae   Well, God know what you like, heh!

King   Hey, hey that ain't fair now!

Camae   The truth ain't gotsta to be fair. It's the truth.

King   But *why* you?

Camae   Believe you me I ain't want this job. First day? Bring over you? The Kang? I ain't wanna do it. But God been gettin' these prayers from a littl'un named Bunny.

A voice flutters out of **Camae***'s mouth like a butterfly. It softly lands inside the room.*

'Please, God, don't let my daddy die alone.' When I heard it . . . Well, it just 'bout broke my heart. I just had to come . . .

Camae *actually does start to cry, and flowers bloom at her feet.*

Beat.

King   You know her nickname . . . Bernice, my sweet Bernice. My baby girl spoke to you?

Camae   Her prayers are powerful. I can tell she's yourn. She gots a way with words. A gift. Soundin' like she gone be a preacher one day. I don't like chiren too much, but she . . . she somethin'.

King   My Bunny, my baby girl. Even she knows . . .

Camae   Yes. I gotta take you to the other side. (*Pause.*) Look, I know you afraid, Preacher Kang –

King   How you know I'm afraid?

Camae   Because . . . You should be.

She points to the door of the motel. Beneath the door burns bright red. The door begins to bulge and wave as fingers begin to push and poke through the door. **King** *slowly walks towards the door, drawn to the danger, drawn to the bullet . . .*

King (*with total calm*)   You talk about fear, Camae, well . . . I have felt fear. Felt it in my guts. Felt it in my toes. Felt it even when I stood in front of my own congregation in my own church. There beneath that old rugged cross, I quaked and shook with fear. My insides churned and I fought hard to keep them from leaping out of my mouth. You see, a Negro man is not safe in a pulpit. Not even in a pulpit of his own making. Sunday mornings have been the mornings when I am most afraid. 'Cause in this country a pulpit is a pedestal and we all know that, in America, the tall tree is felled first. Tall trees have more wood to burn, Camae. We are the sacrifice.

Camae   You been knowin' I was comin', haven't you?

King   Yes. Oh, yes. I have dreamed of you. Rather had nightmares. In my darkest hours, I've even prayed for you with eyes wide open. Been so many death threats that some nights I have asked God, 'Please just get it over with.' Even tonight at the church . . .

He softly cups her face in his hand.

Who knew death would be so beautiful? Almost make a man wanna die.

Camae   You not afraid of me?

King   Fear has become my companion, my lover. I know the touch of fear, even more than I know the touch of my own wife's. Fear, Camae, is my best friend. She is the reason I get up in the morning. 'Cause I know if I'm still afraid, then I am still alive.

Camae   Tomorrow. When it time, you gone have to take my hand.

King   Tomorrow? But I'm not ready to die. I still got so much work to do.

Camae   But God say it time.

King   No, it's not my time. I ain't ready. I still have so much work to do.

He points to the papers back at his desk and he goes to sit down. He writes:

King (*to* **Camae**)   'Why America is going to hell – '

Camae   Preacher Kang, now you / gone have to put that down.

King (*'King voice' back on*)   A country that sends brown boys to bathe little-bitty brown babies in the blood of our greed is headed for a crossroads of conscience. Hurt villages set ablaze by our damning ignorance.

Camae   You hear what I said? You ain't gone be able to finish that, nanh.

King   – And the consequence? Our young are flown back home in star-strangled coffins. Unwashable our hands, as we stand at the stone-cold closed gates of heaven wondering why our God will not let us in.

Camae   Preacher Kang . . .

King   And why won't He?

Camae   *SHE!!*

King   – *She* let us in, my sweet America? 'Cause America is going to hell! Cast down like Lucifer in the pit to burn, baby, burn! I warn you, my America, my sweet America, a tsunami of rage is rolling across the seas and America is surrounded by hot water, waiting to drown.

Camae (*under her breath*)   And I thought *I* was the radical.

King   The rage is rising, my brethren, RISING, like a forever-surging tide as the rich get richer and the poor get poorer. But the children of the Nile will rise, my America. They will RISE!! Pharaohs will be overthrown, cast into those boiling waters of their arrogance! We will rise, my brethren! Can I get an Amen? I *said* can I get an Amen?

Camae   Amen!!

King (*panting, spent from his inspiration*)   See, that'll make a good sermon, won't it?

Camae   Hell, I'd sit in a pew for a few for that one.

King   So you agree with me? Well, I gots to finish my sermon and I need to be alone to finish my sermon so . . . you gone have to fly on away.

He continues scribbling with his pen, fast and furiously.

Camae   King, come on now, you need to come on!

King   Exactly one year ago, I stood in that crumbling pulpit in Riverside and shouted that this war would be our own violent undoing, freedom's suicide . . . Well, I'll tell you, there weren't too many Amens *that* Sunday. But who is a man who does not speak his mind? He is not a man, but I *am* a man. I AM A MAN! If only they could see that love, love is the most radical weapon of destruction there is. Sweet radical love. But they don't get it. Instead, they have call me every name in the book except a child of God. Even my own men: 'You splittin' the movement, Martin, you splittin' the movement! You can't focus on war, and poverty, and Negroes. Choose one!!' But I could not, *will* not choose just –

Camae   But ain't you just a civil rights leader? You can't be talkin' 'bout war, then this, then that.

King   And why the hell not?

Camae   I'm just sayin' I think it's just a bit too much for one man to handle all on his lonesome.

King   Don't you think I know that?

Camae   I don't think you do. Who you thank you is, the President?

King   I think I might wear the suit mighty well.

Camae   Well, I know somebody who wear it better.

King   Better than me? I don't think so.

He goes back to his speech, writing, cutting, editing . . .

(*The 'King voice' again*)   'America is going to hell' . . .

Camae   Preacher Kang, you can't call all the shots, all the time –

King (*under his breath*)   Just for a little bit more time, just a little bit more . . .

Still writing.

America, America –

Camae   Preacher Kang, –

King   *– my country tis of thee –*

Camae   You makin' my job harder –

King   *– my country that doles out constant misery –*

Camae   – harder than it already is –

King   *– war abroad, then war in* your *streets, Arrogant America.*

Camae   – this hard on me.

King (*bolting from his desk*)   Hard on *you*? What about it bein' hard on me? On my family? On Corrie? On the movement? HAS GOD THOUGHT ABOUT THAT?!

Camae   God ain't the one you need to be mad at while you up there yellin'! God ain't the one you need to be blamin' –

King   Then who needs to be blamed?

Camae   It ain't *who* needs to be blamed, Preacher Kang. It's *what*. It ain't a *who*, it's a *what*, Preacher Kang. Evil is not under God's jurisdiction. But good, *good* is.

King   Well, can't you stop it? Catch whatever's coming?

Camae   That ain't my job. God said I gotta get you ready to come on home.

King   But we still got work to do. I got more sermons in me, more goals, more . . . plans!

He gets down on bended knee.

Camae, I wanna do another March on Washington. Bigger. Better. Bolder.

Camae   Another *dream* of yours?

King   But I wanna make *this* one a reality! The plan. It's all in the works. It's called the Poor People's Campaign!

Camae   Poor People's Campaign? What that is? It bet' not be no 'nother march. You / and yo marches.

King   Listen to me.

Camae   You and yo / marches!

King   Please, Camae! Listen!

She sits down on the bed and starts eating popcorn out of her maid's uniform.

Camae   I'm listening. Gone.

King   We've been organizing this campaign all year. All year. Imagine, Camae. On the Washington Mall, not thousands, but millions –

Camae   Millions of Negroes on the Washington Mall? / Shiiiiiit.

King   No, no, not just Negroes. White folk, Chinese folk, Indian folk, all banding together to shame this country. All kinds of poor folks pulling their mule wagons across the Washington Mall. A rainbow of people chanting, 'Stop the war on Vietnam! Start the war on poverty!'

Camae   Unh, unh! How 'bout 'Make love! Not poverty!'?

King   Hey, I like that one, too! They can call me Commie King all they like, I don't care. Poor people matter, Camae. They matter! That's why we had to come here. Not to walk, but to march. Peacefully. Memphis is just a dress rehearsal for the big one. *Memphis* is just the beginning.

Camae   Yo' men'll carry it on.

King   But I'm the leader of this movement. The head of the body.

Camae   Well, the body will just have to grow another head 'cause Memphis is the end of the road for you.

King   End of the road? But . . . but . . . can't you . . . can't you ask God?

Camae   Honey, I can't do you no kinda special / favors!

King   Just till next month? Till I see this plan on through? Just till April 29th.

Camae   And what if She let you? You just gone keep on saying one more day, one more month, one more this, one more that!

King   No, I won't.

Camae   Yes, you will! I know you, Preacher Kang.

King   But I have so much work to do –

Camae   But what about yo' mens? Can't they see it through?

King   They don't dream the same dreams I do, Camae. They think I'm crazy to dream this big, and maybe I am a little crazy, but how can we fight the war in Vietnam but not the wars against Negroes in our streets? How can we try to put a man on the moon but not feed starving children in Mississippi? There's just so much I gotta do. So much I haven't yet accomplished. So much . . . I GOTTA FINISH WHAT I STARTED!!

Camae   It ain't all about you! *You! You!* Gosh, you men are so selfish. They always thank it's 'bout them. Them! *Them!* Hah! Well, let me tell you something, Preacher Kang. Let me tell you! Like most men, you ain't gone be able to finish what you started.

King   My house has been bombed! I have been pelted wit' rocks. My arm twisted behind my back. My face shoved into a ground of gravel. I have been kicked at. Spit at. Pummelled. Abused. Looked at with the deepest scorn. I have been stabbed in my chest. And I walked away. Alive! Alive! If I woulda sneezed I woulda died.

Camae (*under her breath*)   Well, I'm glad you ain't have no cold that day.

King (*ignoring her*)   Look at the life I've lived. You tell me I ain't got favor wit' God! After all that? Tell me I ain't jumped over every hurdle of this race!

Camae   Well, sometimes you done cleared the hurdles and sometimes . . . you ain't. Remember Albany? You done brought us far. But you a man. You just a man, baby. You're not God, though some folk'll say you got mighty close. You know . . . sometimes, you've failed.

Beat. The wind sinks out of his sails.

King   Like when that boy . . . that boy got shot. Larry Payne.

Camae   Well, *that* wun't yo' fault. Police killed that boy. Not you.

Beat. **Camae** *stands silent.*

King   . . . So this motel room will become my tomb? But I have survived so much . . .

Camae   Honey, I know all about your trials and tribulations. I done read yo' blessings file. It bigger than yo' FBI file and that bigga than the Bible. I know it might be hard for you to leave this life . . . yo' family . . . and all yo' plans. But you gone have to pass off that baton, little man. You in a relay race, albeit the fastest runner we done ever seen't. But you 'bout to burn out, superstar. You gone need to pass off that baton . . .

Beat.

King   I know I have dropped this baton so many times over this race. But I promise, I ain't gonna do it again. Tell Her.

Camae   *Tell* Her?

King   Yes, tell Her I promise, I won't ever drop this baton again. Tell Her, She needs to let me stay. Ask Her. For me.

Camae (*hissing*)   You ain't supposed to question God. That's the rule. You know that!

King   There ain't no rules for an angel like you!

Camae   Shhiiiit! God gots rules! I had to read the whole Bible today –

King   Please. Camae.

Camae   Dr. KANG!

King   PLEASE!!

Pause.

Camae   Well . . . whatchoo gone give *me*?

King (*smiles seductively*)   A kiss from the Kang.

Camae   I don't want no kiss from you, 'cause you ain't brushed yo' teeth.

King   Please, Camae . . .

He goes down on bended knee. He plucks one of the flowers from the carpet and hands it to her in submission. Beat.

Camae (*disgusted*)   Ughhh.

She snatches it from him. She walks over to the rotary phone on the night stand beside the bed. She dials a really long phone number.

You lucky I 'member this. This just my first day.

She waits and waits . . . and waits. Finally, someone on the other end picks up. **King** *sits beside* **Camae** *and tries to listen in on the conversation.*

Camae   Hey, St Augustine. What up? Yeah . . . Can I speak to God? (*Beat.*) What She doin'? (*Pause.*) Ohhhh . . . (*To* **King**.) There are some forest fires. She had to go make some rain and – (*To St Augustine.*) Unh, hunh. When She gone be back? Well . . . Can you call her cell phone? 'Cause this man is really gettin' on my nerves. I'm tryin' to get him on the program. Yeah, I KNOW!! That's what I tried to tell him. You know . . . Martyrs. (*Pause.*) Sho' can. (*To* **King**.) He tryin' to get her on the cell.

King   The cell?

Camae   It's like . . . a phone that ain't got no cord.

King   A phone wit' no cord?

Camae   Sorta like when you talkin' to God. Don't need no real cord, She just sorta . . . answers –

Beat. She perks up. Someone has come to the phone.

Camae   Hello there, God. It's me. Camae. Mmmhmmm. How it goin'? (*She looks at* **King**.) It goin' pretty good. Yep. Yeah, I'm halfway through my shift. Taking a break . . . but . . . uhm . . . Well, there's a bit of problem. He found out. (*She pulls the phone away from her ear.*) I know . . . I know . . . but there's worser news: he say he ain't ready. (*God yells at her ass again.*) That what I told him. I know . . . I know . . . I KNOW.

King   Let me talk to Her.

Camae   No –

King   I wanna talk to yo' supervisor!

Camae *puts her hand over the phone.*

Camae   Shhh! I'm tryin' to butter Her up first.

King   Butter Her up? Let me talk to Her!!

He tries to snatch the phone from **Camae**.

Camae   Hold on a got gum minute, Preacher Kang! (*Pause.*) Yes. But he stubborn! (*She looks at him.*) And quite convincing. He sho'll do got a way wit' words. I know you told me. You wanna talk to him? Well, good. 'Cause he wanna talk to You.

She hands the phone over to him. **King** *snatches it. Clears his throat. Puts the phone to his ear. Beat.*

King   Uhm. God? It's uhmm . . . (*Putting on his 'King voice'.*) Dr. Martin Luther King, J – oh, yes. Michael, to you . . . Yes Ma'am . . . yes Ma'am . . . yes . . . Ma'am. (*He pulls the phone from his ear and whispers.*) Is She –

Camae   Black? Mmhm. And PROUD . . .

King *puts the phone back to his ear.*

King   God, Ma'am, You don't sound like I thought You'd
sound. No, no, no. Pardon me, if that offends. I like how You
sound. Kinda like my grandmama. Well . . . it is a compliment. I
loved her dearly . . . I love You more, though. Camae told me
that you might be busy tonight. Oh, You have time for me? For
one of Your favorites?

He smiles at **Camae**, *who rolls her eyes.*

King   God, are You all right? You sound hoarse. Oh, You
tired? Well, it must be tiring to be everywhere all at the same
time (*He laughs nervously.*) Well, God . . . I don't mean to trouble
You, Ma'am, but I wanted to ask You something . . . You see I
have always listened to You, honored Your word, lived by Your
word – (*He lowers his voice.*) for the most part – (*Raises it back to
normal.*) God, please don't strike me down for askin' this, but . . .
I want to live. I have plans. Lots of plans in my head and in
my heart and my people need me. They need me. And I need
to see them to the Promised Land. (*Beat.*) I know that's not
what I said earlier tonight, I know, but . . . I wasn't lying
exactly. (*He looks at* **Camae**.) I just didn't know she was comin'
so, so . . . soon. I meant every word I said tonight when I spoke
to those people. Dead honest! No, not like that! . . . God, I just
. . . I want to see my people there, the tide is turning . . . war is
becoming the order of the day and I must, I must convince
them to be vigilant . . . We've come too far to turn back now . . .
God, listen to me . . . Who else is betta fit for this job? I mean,
who will take my place? (*He hears Her answer.*) JESSE?! (*Pause.*) I –
I – I just thought Ralph would make a better – No, no, no, no,
I have not turned vain. On the contrary. I'm but a servant for
You, God, Ma'am. Yes, I've been a servant for You all my life.
At one point in time, I might nota been up for the challenge
but I knew this was all par for the course and I did Your will.
I honored YOUR WILL, God, Ma'am. Let me not die a man
who doesn't get to hug his children one last time. Let me not
die a man who never gets to make love to his wife one last
time. Let me not be a man who dies afraid and alone. (*Long

pause.) Then why'd You pick me, huh? Hmm, no disrespect, but if You didn't know what I could do, what my (*hissing*) *talents* were then . . . You got some nerve. Dragging me here to this moldy motel room in Memphis. To die. HUH! Of all places! Well, I *am* angry. There have been many a' nights when I have held my tongue when it came to You. But not tonight, NOT TONIGHT. I have continuously put my life on the line, gave it all up. Gave it all up for You and Your word. You told me, that'd I'd be safe. Safe in Your arms. You protected me all this time, all this time! Glued a pair of wings to my back, but now that've I've flown too close to the sun I'm falling into the ocean of death. God how dare You take me now? NOW! I beg of You. I plead – God? Ma'am? God?

Long heavy silence.

Camae (*whispers from the corner*)   What She say?

King   I think . . . I think she hung up on me.

Camae   Hmm. Coulda been a dropped call.

Pause.

King   A dropped call? How does one 'drop' a call? This angel talk you speak . . .

Camae   You act like I'm speakin' in tongues.

King   Well, you speak of things I know nothing about.

Camae   Yes. I speak of the future.

King   The future?

Camae   Angels are everywhere and nowhere. Any time and any place. We speak all languages. In all times. *Ne mogu poverit chto ti zastavil menya eto sdelat!! (Russian translation: I can't believe you made me do that.) Niwe oha. Noza kureta ebizibu. (Runyankole translation: I don't know who you think you are. You're going to get me in trouble!)*

Then she growls extremely convincingly as a dog. Translation: I'ma bite your fucking head off.

(*Aggressively.*) Ooooo!! YOU DONE GOT ME IN TROUBLE!! God gone tan my hide from brown to barbecue.

King   How did I get *you* in trouble?

Camae   Look, I can't just call Her for you! You gone make me lose my wings.

She rubs her breasts.

King   Good, you need to lose them! Maybe you'll stop luring men to their deaths! (*Pause.*) I can't believe She hung up on me.

Camae   I woulda hung up on you, too. Yellin' like that.

King   God hung up on me. She forsook her servant.

Camae   She ain't forsake you neither. She just ain't wanna hear yo' shit. She got the right. She is God, ya know?

King   And I am Dr. King, *ya know?*

Beat.

Camae   Don't mark me, man . . .

King   *Ya know? Ya know?*

Camae   I do *not* sound like that.

King   Least you don't say, ya dig? *Ya dig? Ya dig?* Like a Black Panther Party angel! That's how you would sound if you said it, too. *Ya dig?*

Camae   Ohhh.

She picks up a pillow lying on the bed and pelts him with it.

King   Camae! God gonna get you. Beatin' up one of Her favorites like this!

Camae   Can't believe she done sent me to come get you witcho crazy ass.

She pelts him with a pillow again and again. **King** *picks up a pillow to protect himself. She misses him this time. Laughs heartily.*

Camae   You thank you so funny, Preacher Man.

King   That's right! Hit me! Hit me if you think you bad!

He is quick and surprisingly good at pillow-fighting. He clobbers her over the head with the pillow.

Camae   OW!

King   That's what you get for battling the Kang of pillow-fightin'!

He pummels her again with the pillow. She flies across the bed.

Camae   You can't hit angels with pillows!

King   Where is that rule?

Camae   In the Bible!

King   Unh, unh! Where?

Camae   Ezekiel, fool!

She clobbers him one good time. He falls on to the bed. Her pillow bursts and feathers flutter out. Spilling across the room. He hits her back, and his pillow bursts. More feathers fly across the room. They laugh. They laugh as feathers are falling. Falling everywhere like the rain was before and the snow was before. There is a feather blizzard inside Room 306 at the Lorraine Motel. And **King** *and his death angel roll in the feather storm of their own making. Their pillows, now devoid of fluff, are tossed to the wayside and then* **King** *takes* **Camae** *and starts tickling her.*

Camae   Stop it!

King   I bet you're ticklish.

Camae   Don't tickle me!

King   Why?

Camae   'Cause I'ma pee on you!

King   Angels don't pee.

Camae   Try me. That's in the Bible, too.

King   No, it's not!

Camae   Watch out, my piss gone burn you! Tsssss!

King   I don't believe you.

Camae   You betta!

He tickles her.

I'm peein'! STOP! I'm peein'!

He finally somehow pins **Camae** *on to her back. He is on top of her. They stop. Gazing into each other's eyes. Out of breath. A bit sweaty.*

King   I never thought death would be so beautiful.

Camae   Sometimes. Tonight's a good night. I remembered my rouge.

Beat.

King   Camae?

Camae   Yes, Preacher Kang.

King   Hold me.

Beat. **King***'s eyes well with tears and this strong, grown man dissolves into the child no one ever saw. He slides down on top of her. Crying. Crying his heart out. Sobbing. And* **Camae** *holds him. And rubs his back as if he were a child.*

Camae (*softly*)   There . . . there . . . let it all out. Give it all to me. I will take it all . . . there . . . there . . . give it all to me.

King (*hiccupping like children do*)   I've been prayin' that it would stop.

Camae   There . . . there . . . / Shhhh.

King   That it would all go away. I never wanted to do this. I just wanted to be a minister in my small church.

Camae   But when your maker calls you, you must heed the call.

King   I just wanted to be a minister. That was enough. That was enough . . .

Camae   But God had bigger plans for you.

King   Why me?

Camae   Why not you?

King   'Cause I'm . . . just a man. I know now, I know. And it's time for me to come on home. Help me. Help me get my things together.

He rises and heads to his suitcase. He begins to pack it.

Camae   You won't be needing that. Won't be needing that at all. Heaven got all you need.

King *looks around the room.*

King   Well . . . I need to leave my men some instructions. Notes.

Camae   They can do it on they own.

King   But I need to tell them what to do when I'm . . . gone.

Camae   They'll know what to do. You've taught them well.

Soft pause.

King   Well . . . well . . . my wife . . . I need to call my wife . . .

He runs to the phone and dials. He sings into it again.

Corrie pick up. Corrie pick up. Corrie, Corrie Corrie pick up.

She doesn't pick up. Silence. He finally hangs up the phone. Long heavy beat.

I always bought her flowers when I went away. Always with the mind that they would last long enough till I made it home. Sometimes they would. Most times they didn't. I could never make amends, so I bought her flowers that would stand in for those passin' pockets of time just as I existed for her. I picked a beautiful flower called 'absence'. And it bloomed like dandelions, a weed she could never rid her garden of. Last week, when I was home, I walked past this shop, and I saw the most perfect flowers. Radiant red carnations. I went into the store, and, you know what I found out, Camae? They weren't real. My eyes had fooled me. But I bought those flowers, and they arrived yesterday morning just before I boarded the plane to Memphis. She came to me, with a twinkle in her eyes and said, 'Why, Martin. You never give me these old artificial things . . . ' I smiled. 'Today is different. Today . . . '

Camae   You knew she'd need a flower that could last forever.

King   If only I could tell them how sorry I am. If only I could have been there with them. I missed birthdays. I missed holidays. I –

Camae   You did what you had to do. We needed you. The world needed you.

King   Many a times I've wanted to quit. To give up the ghost.

Camae   But you didn't. You prevailed.

King   I don't know for what! I've sacrificed my marriage, my family. My health. For what?

Camae   Powerful the man that get more done dead than alive.

King   But I don't want to be a martyr.

Camae   That suit fits you well.

King   I am a man. I am just a man.

Camae   Tomorrow, you'll be a man made martyr. No, better yet! A saint!

King   Don't call me that. I'm a sinner, not a saint. I'm not deservin' of the title.

Camae   You think I am?

King   You must. God must a' been impressed with how you've lived your life –

Camae (*quietly*)   No . . . She wun't.

She turns away.

King   But I thought angels were perfect.

Camae   You perfect?

King   No.

Camae   Then why should I be? Honey, I've robbed. I've
lied. I've cheated. I've failed. I've cursed. But what I'm
ashamed of most is, I've hated. Hated myself. Sacrificed my
flesh so that others might feel whole again. I thought it was my
duty. All that I had to offer this world. What else was a poor
black woman, the mule of the world, here for? Last night, in
the back of a alley I breathed my last breath. A man clasped
his hands like a necklace 'round my throat. I stared into his big
blue eyes, as my breath got ragged and raw, and I saw the hell
this old world had put him through. The time he saw his father
hang a man. The time he saw his mother raped. I felt so sorry
for him. I saw what the world had done to him, and I still
couldn't forgive. I hated him for stealing my breath. When I
passed on to the other side, God – ooooo, She is more
gorgeous than me. She the color of midnight and Her eyes are
brighter than the stars. Her hair . . . well . . . just you wait till
you see her hair – God stood there before me. With this look
on her face. I just knowed She was just soooo disappointed in
me. I was just a' cryin', weepin' at her feet. Beggin' her not to
throw me down. All that sinnin'. All that grime on my soul. All
that hatred in my heart. But then I looked up and saw that She
was smilin' down at me. She opened her mouth, and silence
came out. But I heard her loud and clear. 'I got a special task
for you and if you complete it, all your sins will be washed
away.'

I opened my file. And I saw my task was you. What could little
old me, give to big old you? I thought you was gone be perfect.
Well, you ain't, but then you are. You have the biggest heart I
done ever knownt. You have the strength to love those who
could never love you back. If I had just a small fraction of the

love you have for this world, then maybe, just maybe I could become half the angel you are.

Long heavy beat.

King   Will I die at the hands of a white man, too?

Beat.

Camae   Yes. Speak by love. Die by hate.

King   Where will it be?

Camae   On the balcony just right there.

They look to the door of the room.

King   How?

Camae   Surrounded by those who love you.

King   Will you be there to clean up the mess?

Camae   It would be an honor, Preacher Kang.

King   Will there be others after me? To carry on the baton.

Camae   Many, many will carry it on, but there'll never be another you. You are a once-in-a-lifetime affair.

King   Is the future as beautiful as you?

Camae   Yes . . . and it's as ugly as me, too.

King   I wanna see it.

Camae   I don't know if you could handle it. It might break your heart.

King   My heart already weary, Camae. I wanna see it before I die.

Camae   But I thought you done already seen the Promised Land?

King   In my dreams, but I wanna see it with my eyes. My own eyes. If I see – *really* see it, I will die a happy man tomorrow. I will go willingly into your arms, Camae. If you just let me see these dreams I'll never ever see.

Beat.

A trembling **King** *reaches out to* **Camae**. *She doesn't take his hand.*

Camae   I'll let you see, but when you're called back you'll have to come. I'ma have to take you on home tomorrow.

King   What time shall I meet you?

Camae   6:01 p.m.

King   Is it gonna hurt?

Camae   You won't feel the hurt. The world will.

King (*teary eyed*) You promise?

Camae   I promise. You ready?

King *nods, gulping back tears.*

Camae   Let's take you to the mountaintop.

She walks up to him and kisses him. He becomes woozy in her arms. She stares at him. Lightning flickers as images from that fateful day, 4 April 1968, begin to seep through the hotel walls.

Camae
  The Prince of Peace. Shot.
  His blood stains the concrete outside Room 306
  A worker wipes away the blood but not before
  Jesse baptizes his hands on the balcony
  The baton passes on

More and more images of the American experience consume the walls as the world begins to disintegrate right before their very eyes.

  Memphis burning
  DC burning
  Cities burning
  Vietnam burning
  Coffins coming home

Another Kennedy killed
The baton passes on

Bayard Rustin
Stonewall Riots
Andrew Young
Julian Bond
Bob Marley
Redemption Songs
Angela Davis
Assatta Shakur
Afro picks
Black raised fists
Olympics
The baton passes on

*The images have picked up in speed and the world continues to float away.
It's almost as if* **King** *is surrounded by the images, walking through the
future that he will never inhabit.*

Camae
White children
Black children
Crayola-color children
Together in a cafeteria

Roots
The Jeffersons
Sidney Poitier
Superfly
Isaac Hayes
James Brown
I'm black and I'm PROUD!
Jesse for President
I am Somebody!

Camae *begins to float away into another world. Another dimension.
Her voice becoming an echo as the future continues to consume the stage.*

Camae
Crips

Bloods
Blue
Red
White
Crack
Smack
Marion Barry
Tracks
AIDS
Reagan wins again

Berlin Walls
Apartheid falls
Robben Island sets Mandela free
Rodney King screams:
'Can't we all just get along?'
The baton passes on

No peace in the Middle East
Ruby Dee
'You sho'll is ugly!'
Spike Lee
Rwanda bleeds
Bill Clinton
Niggah please

Skinheads
The Cosby Show
Baby Mamas
Soul Train
Montelle
Don't Ask Don't Tell

Run DMC
BET
MTV
Walk this way
The baton passes on

And on and on
Till the break of dawn
For the American song
We shall overcome

A white Bronco flees into the night
If it doesn't fit, you must acquit

James Byrd
Columbine
Ron Brown
Colin Powell
Clarence Thomas
Tupac
Oprah
Biggie
Crack Corners
From Crenshaw
To MLK Boulevard

Saddam Hussein
Osama
George Bush
Condi Rice

The Towers sigh
The world turns gray
September 11th
One bright morning day

Katrina, Katrina
American as apple pie
Drove the Chevy to the levee
But the levee was drowned
The Superdome

Drive-bys
McDonald's
Diabetes
Iraq
NBA

High-paid slaves
The children of the Nile
A nuclear 8 Mile
Black picket fences
And Jena Six
American flags
And Black Presidents!!!

The baton passes on
The baton passes on
The baton passes on
The baton passes on

The good, the bad and the ugly of America continue to proceed like a fluid mental freeway into the very edge of now and perhaps beyond. It's like a river with no levee and the images flood our senses, our mind, and our heart. The sound and the fury of it all rises to a frenetic peak until BOOM! CRICKLE! CRICKLE-CRACK!! A flash of lightning illuminates the stage. And suddenly **King** *stands in the deep dark blue of the blackness, trying to take his rightful place in the universe among the stars. He is looking over our heads. Past us, through us, floating above us in the silence.*

King (*in utter amazement*)   What is this vision I see before me? Could this be my wildest dream? (*Taking it all in.*) There it is. There. It. Is. A land where hunger is no more. A land where war is no more. A land where richness is no more, poverty is no more, color is . . . no more. Destruction . . . is no more. Only love. Radical, fierce love. I have spent many years walking through the desert of life. Met oasis after oasis, only to bend my tongue to the waters of justice and have it all disappear before my thirst is quenched. Is this just another mirage, I see before me, Camae? Or is it real?

Camae (*offstage, echoing in the distance*)   It is.

King *takes a step forward towards the lip of blackness until he can go no further. He reaches his trembling hand to touch the faraway vision. He struggles and he struggles to reach it, but he cannot. He cannot. He stands there in awe, tears streaming down his face.*

King   I accept. I will never walk through that blessed garden over yonder . . . that lush land just on that far side of the moon. It . . . is . . . so . . .

He begins to choke back tears.

Oh, Lord, give them strength to walk forward into Canaan, where no matter if you live in a mansion or Madison Avenue or a housing project on MLK Boulevard, you belong in this world, where no matter who you love, love is your inalienable right, where no matter the color of your skin you . . . can . . . achieve . . . anything because we are all children of the Nile and we can no longer wander through this desert with willowed backs.

Walk towards the Promised Land, my America, my sweet America with this baton I give to you, this baton I shall no longer carry. Because you are the climbers, the new carriers of the cross. I beg you, implore you, don't give in and toss it off. On this here mountaintop there is beauty to behold. America, my America in black, red, white, blue, brown and gold. Canaan is calling! Calling for you to come . . . Oh, America, my America, your Promised Land is so close, and yet so far away, so close and yet so far away, so close and yet so –

In a small pinpoint of light **Camae***'s hand comes from behind* **King***, settling on his trembling shoulder.*

Camae   Time.

King *closes his eyes, takes an audible deep breath and –*

Blackout.

Afterword *by James Dacre*

American Words, British Production

This was a cocktail shaken by Katori on one side of the Atlantic and stirred by her on the other.

Four years ago a young actress and I worked together on an unpaid workshop production in New York. She had just graduated from Harvard; I was studying at Columbia University on a Fulbright scholarship, and we were both getting to know the Big Apple. We'd meet late in the evening once she'd finished work and rehearse – in a cupboard, a corridor, even outdoors – until the early hours. Afterwards over drinks she'd talk about writing a play. Was this unusual? No. Thousands of young theatre-makers across the city were doing the same – the only difference was that Katori Hall actually wrote her play.

On Sunday that play – *The Mountaintop* – won Best New Play at the Olivier Awards for its world premiere in London. It was developed and produced under exactly the same circumstances – and with exactly the same spirit – as our first project together. Great reckonings do indeed come in small rooms.

The Mountaintop was developed in New York but – despite trekking the script around numerous theatres – wasn't able to find a home there. Nobody wanted to risk producing a play about one of America's most revered heroes by an unknown writer born fourteen years after he was assassinated. The journey of the play – from Memphis to London, and now on to Broadway – speaks volumes about the culture of new writing in America: a land rich in incentives to create and develop work but lacking in opportunities to have it produced.

The quality of new writing in America is extremely high at the moment. In particular, there is a trend towards theatrically expressive work that engages and ignites an actor's imagination. Yet many of America's most promising playwrights are having their work produced abroad. American theatre has great respect for its young playwrights, but not enough confidence in them. The irony is that since there is so much energy and so little financial stability on the fringe I discovered enormous enthusiasm amongst New York's downtown theatre community for making things happen on their own terms.

And there are surprising advantages to the American system. American writers who grow up in a climate of play readings and workshops, and have to wait years until their work is actually produced learn to treat the rehearsal room as a laboratory – a space open to experiment and risk – rather than somewhere to 'get things done' in time for opening night.

I returned to London last year inspired by this attitude and determined to make *The Mountaintop* work. In Theatre503 I found a company enterprising enough to take a chance on the play and all the uncertainty that came with it. Luck also played its part. On his way home from our first meeting, David Harewood decided to take the role when he saw on the Tube floor – as a sign from the angels – an empty pack of Pall Mall cigarettes: the very same that Martin Luther King smoked.

Theatre503 understood that developing a play is one thing but that doing it is quite another. With the input of an exceptional design team, the very supportive Theatre503 and two uniquely creative actors (Lorraine Burroughs playing the role of Camae), the script and vision of the show evolved in rehearsals. The result was a cocktail shaken by Katori on one side of the Atlantic and stirred by her on the other.

Thankfully we live in a time where there's a lot of theatrical exchange between the US and UK. There's a hunger and enthusiasm for cross-cultural perspectives in both countries' theatre industries. May that flourish still further.

This article originally appeared in the Independent, *23 March 2010*